MAKING
Gift Boxes

Written and Illustrated by
Linda Hendry

KIDS CAN PRESS

Published in Canada by
Kids Can Press Ltd.
29 Birch Avenue
Toronto, ON M4V 1E2

Published in the U.S. by
Kids Can Press Ltd.
85 River Rock Drive, Suite 202
Buffalo, NY 14207

Edited by Laurie Wark
Designed by Karen Powers

Printed in Hong Kong by Wing King Tong Co. Ltd.

CM 99 0 9 8 7 6 5 4 3 2 1

Canadian Cataloguing in Publication Data

Hendry, Linda
    Making gift boxes

(Kids can do it)
ISBN 1-55074-503-4

1. Box craft – Juvenile literature. 2. Ornamental boxes – Juvenile literature. 3. Box making – Juvenile literature. 4. Handicraft – Juvenile literature. I. Title. II. Series.

TT870.5.H46 1999   j745.54   C99-930071-7

Kids Can Press is a Nelvana company.

Contents

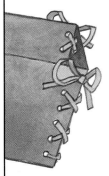

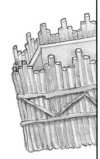

Introduction

This book won't show you how to become a magician, but it will tell you how to work magic on a cracker box to turn it into a fierce-looking monster. And you'll learn how to transform a juice box into a cozy little cottage. Not to live in, of course, but to keep jewelry or other treasures in. This book will show you how to turn easily found items into wonderful little boxes. Boxes not only for storage, or for giving gifts, but boxes to give as gifts themselves.

MATERIALS

Look around your home and you'll find most of the things you will need to make the boxes in this book.

Cardboard

You will need corrugated cardboard and light cardboard. Corrugated cardboard boxes are used to ship heavy things like tins of food. Ask for a box at a supermarket. Cereal or crackers come in boxes made from light cardboard.

Glue

White, non-toxic glue is strong and dries clear.

Measuring

Measurements for each project are given in both metric and imperial, which differ slightly. Choose one measurement system and use it for the entire project.

Scissors and Utility Knives

You can do most of the cutting in this book using a pair of sharp scissors, but you will get a straighter edge if you use a utility knife and a metal-edged ruler. Ask an adult to help you if you use a utility knife. Protect the surface you are cutting on with a piece of corrugated cardboard. Make several light cuts with the knife rather than pressing hard.

It is easier to fold cardboard and heavy paper if you score the fold lines first. To score, lay a metal ruler along the line to be folded and make a very light cut along the edge of the ruler with a utility knife. Do not cut completely through the cardboard or paper.

Paints and Brushes

Acrylic craft paints are inexpensive and come in many colors. They dry quickly, so place only as much as you will need on a piece of waxed paper. Protect your work surface with newspaper.

Small, pointed brushes are best for painting detail. Flat, straight-edged brushes are good for painting larger areas or applying papier mâché. Clean your brushes with water between each color and when you are finished painting.

Decorating techniques

PAPIER-MÂCHÉ

Papier-mâché will strengthen your box and provide a good surface for painting and decorating.

1. Mix 12 spoonfuls of flour, 12 spoonfuls of water and 3 spoonfuls of salt into a smooth paste. (This mixture will keep for several days, covered and refrigerated.)

2. Dip small strips of newspaper into the paste and smooth them onto your box in layers. Continue, covering a small portion at a time, until the entire box is covered in two or three layers.

3. A final layer of tissue-paper strips will give your box a smooth surface. Apply the paste onto the box with a paintbrush, add a layer of tissue strips, and use the brush to smooth them out.

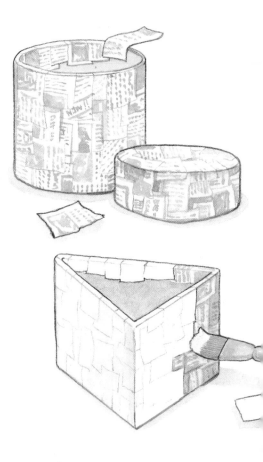

NOTE ABOUT LIDS

If your box has a lid that fits snugly, set the lid in place before you begin and draw a line around the edge of the lid. Set the lid aside and apply the papier-mâché strips below the line. (If you wrap the strips over the rim of the box, the lid might not fit later.)

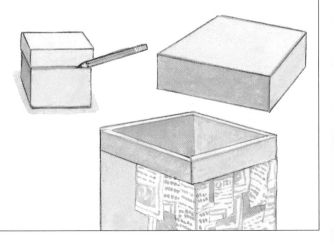

COLLAGE

Magazine pictures, postage stamps, gift wrap or colorful bits of torn paper arranged in a mosaic pattern make an interesting collage finish for your box. You might want to plan your design before you begin gluing.

1. Mix 6 spoonfuls of white glue with 3 spoonfuls of water. Use a paintbrush to spread glue mixture onto a small area of your box.

2. Apply the pictures or paper, wrapping them neatly around the edges of the box opening. Continue until your box is covered.

3. Brush on a final layer of glue mixture to seal the collage. It will dry clear.

PAINT

Apply paint to your box with a brush, a sponge, a crumpled plastic bag or your fingers! Cut designs into a potato, an eraser or a cork, dip them into paint, then stamp the designs onto your box.

DECORATIONS

Buttons, beads, yarn, pasta, dried beans or sea shells. You can glue almost anything to your box to decorate it. If your box has a lid, keep decorations below it.

LINING YOUR BOX

1. Cut a piece of fabric, felt or paper into a strip as wide as the box and as long as the combined measurements of the sides and the bottom of the box. Glue it inside your box.

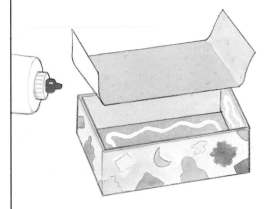

2. Cut a second piece of fabric to criss-cross over the first and cover the opposite sides of the box.

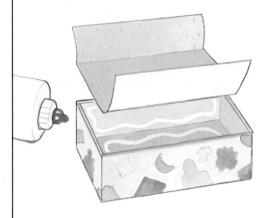

3. Cover the inside of the lid in the same way.

MAKING COMPARTMENTS

1. Cut two strips of light cardboard to fit inside the box from corner to corner.

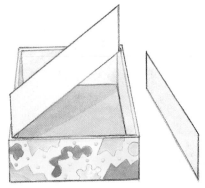

2. Make a cut halfway down in the middle of each strip, then slide the strips together to form an X.

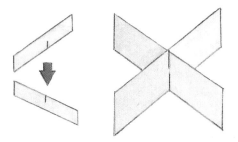

3. Place the strips inside the box to make four compartments. Paint each compartment a different color if you like.

Making boxes

You can make these boxes in any size, just use a larger or smaller cardboard strip and change the measurements as needed.

YOU WILL NEED

- corrugated cardboard (use light cardboard for a circular box),
one piece 7.5 cm x 30 cm (3 in. x 12 in.),
one piece 2.5 cm x 38 cm (1 in. x 15 in.),
and one piece 15 cm x 25 cm
(6 in. x 10 in.)

- papier-mâché (see page 6)

- a pencil, a ruler, a utility knife or scissors, masking tape

A SQUARE BOX

1. Divide the widest cardboard strip into four sections, each 7.5 cm (3 in.) wide. Score each section, fold into a box shape and hold it with tape.

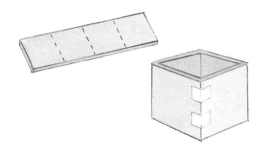

2. To make a bottom, place the box onto the large piece of cardboard and trace around the edge. Cut out the shape.

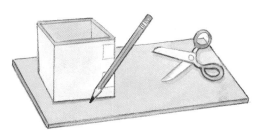

3. To make a top for the lid, trace around the bottom piece. Cut just outside the lines you drew, making a top shape slightly larger than the bottom shape.

Instructions continue on the next page ☞

4. For the sides of the lid, place the top shape at the left end of the long narrow strip, lining up the bottom edges. Draw a line along the right side of the square.

5. Line up the left side of the top shape with the line you drew. Draw a line along the right side.

6. Repeat step 5 two more times and trim off the small section at the end. You should have four equal sections. Score each section, fold into a square shape and tape the top to it.

7. Tape the bottom of the box in place.

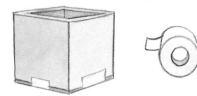

A TRIANGLE BOX

1. Follow steps 1 to 3 for making a square box, but divide the widest cardboard strip into three sections, each 10 cm (4 in.) wide.

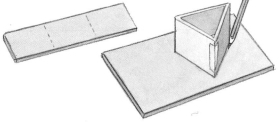

2. To make the sides of the lid, place the larger triangle at one end of the long narrow strip, lining up the bottom edge. Mark the length of the triangle. Repeat two more times.

Draw a line straight up from each point you marked and trim off the small section at the end. You should have three equal sections. Score each section, fold into a triangle shape and tape the top to it.

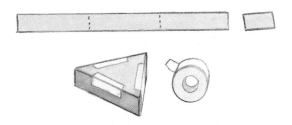

3. Tape the bottom of the box in place.

A CIRCULAR BOX

1. Bend the widest strip of light cardboard into a circle or oval. Overlap the ends about 2.5 cm (1 in.) and tape in place.

3. For the sides of the lid, bend the narrow strip around the top of the box, overlap the ends, trim them slightly and tape in place. The strip should easily slide up and down the outside of the box.

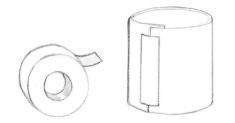

2. To make a bottom, place the box onto the large piece of cardboard, trace around the edge, cut out the shape and tape it in place.

4. To make a top for the lid, place the lid strip on the cardboard, trace around it, cut out the shape and tape it in place.

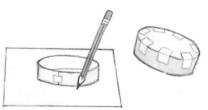

When your box is made, you can cover it with a layer of papier-mâché, then paint or decorate it.

Chest-of-drawers box

This little dresser is a great place to store jewelry or small trinkets.

YOU WILL NEED

- 4 large matchboxes
- 2 sheets of gift wrap in complementary colors
- a darning needle
- 4 pieces of wool, each about 20 cm (8 in.) long
- 8 large beads
- paint, a paintbrush, scissors, glue

1 Slide the drawers out of the matchboxes and set them aside. Paint around the edges of both ends of each box. This will give your box a nice, finished look.

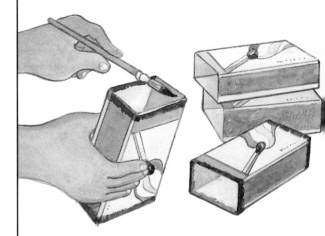

2 Cut or tear one sheet of gift wrap into small pieces and use collage (see page 7) to cover the top and one side of each box. Do not wrap paper over the edges of the openings. Let the boxes dry.

3 Using small pieces of the second sheet of gift wrap, cover both ends of each drawer in collage. Neatly wrap the side, bottom and top edges of the drawer fronts. Let them dry.

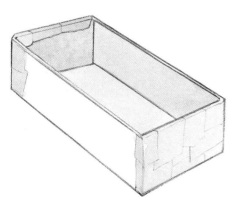

4 Spread glue on each unpapered side of each box and assemble them as shown.

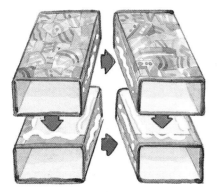

5 Thread a piece of wool onto the needle and carefully push it through a drawer front from inside. Thread a bead onto the wool, then push the needle back through the drawer front, pulling the bead tight. Tie a knot, trim the ends, then secure the knot with a dab of glue. Repeat with the remaining drawers. Insert the drawers into the dresser.

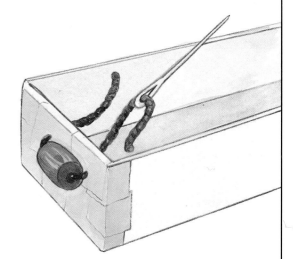

6 To make legs for your dresser, glue a bead in each corner on the bottom.

Photo box

A box for storing photos makes a great gift. Instead of using pictures from newspapers, photocopy photos of your family or friends.

YOU WILL NEED

- a 10 cm x 15 cm (4 in. x 6 in.) photo
- a shoebox
- a piece of corrugated cardboard the same size as the box lid
- a piece of light cardboard the same size as the box lid
- brown paper (lunch-bag paper works well)
- photos from newspapers or magazines
- masking tape, ruler, pencil, utility knife or scissors, white glue, a paintbrush

1 To make the frame, tape the photo in the center of the corrugated cardboard. The space around the photo should be the same on opposite sides. Trace around the photo.

2 From the light cardboard, cut two strips as wide as the space at the sides of the photo and as long as the side of the box. Cut a third strip as wide and as long as the space at the bottom of the photo. Set the strips aside.

3 Remove the photo from the lid and, inside the rectangle, draw a second rectangle that is 0.5 cm (¼ in.) smaller on all sides. Cut out the smaller rectangle.

4 Using collage (see page 7), cover the front of the frame with a layer of brown-paper strips, neatly wrapping all edges.

5 Cover the sides and top edges of the box lid in brown-paper strips. Let the frame and lid dry.

6 Collage the clipped photos to the box, wrapping the photos over the top and bottom edges. Let the box dry.

7 Glue the light-cardboard strips to the lid of the box, lining up the outside edges. Let them dry for an hour, then apply glue to the strips. Place the frame on the lid, set a heavy book on top and let the glue dry.

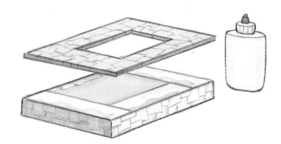

8 Slide the photo into the frame and place the lid on the box.

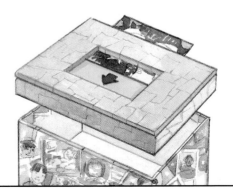

Treasure box

This box has two compartments, each with a false bottom for hiding away important documents or secret treasure maps.

YOU WILL NEED

- 2 same-sized tissue boxes
- light cardboard from one large cereal box (or equivalent)
- 2 pieces of felt or fabric, each 13 cm x 25 cm (5 in. x 10 in.)
- 2 pieces of bristol board, 1 piece 23 cm x 30 cm (9 in. x 12 in.), 1 piece 5 cm x 30 cm (2 in. x 12 in.)
- a hole punch
- 2 brass fasteners, each 2.5 cm (1 in.) long
- scissors, a ruler and pencil, glue

1 Cut the top off one tissue box, leaving a 1 cm (½ in.) border all round. This will be the bottom of your box.

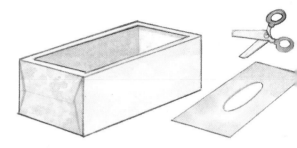

2 To make the lid, cut the top off the second tissue box then cut the top half off each long side. Cut each short side in a semicircle shape.

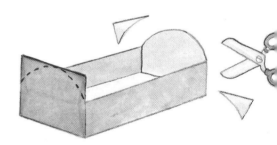

3 Trace each side of the boxes onto the light cardboard. Cut out the pieces and glue them to the insides of the boxes to strengthen them.

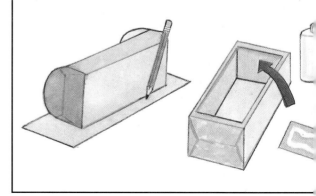

4 To make the false bottoms, trace the boxes onto light cardboard and cut the pieces out. Cut and glue a piece of felt to each cardboard piece. Make two tabs from leftover felt, glue one to each cardboard piece, and set them inside the boxes.

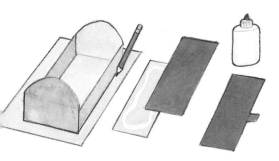

5 If you like, cover the boxes in a layer of papier-mâché or collage (see pages 6 to 7) and decorate the boxes before continuing.

6 Line up one long side of the large piece of bristol board with the edge of the lid and fold it over to the front. Mark the point where it meets the edge and trim to fit. Trim each short side so that it slightly overlaps the lid.

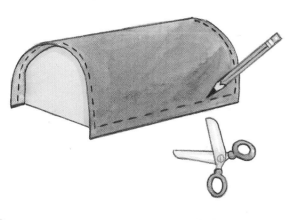

7 To make a hinge, trim the strip of bristol board to the same length as the box, fold it in half lengthwise and unfold. Set the lid on the box, lining up all sides. Glue the strip of paper to the boxes, as shown.

8 Apply glue to the top half of the hinge and attach the large piece of bristol board, as shown.

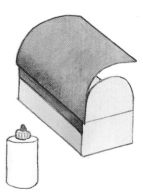

9 Use the hole punch to make two holes near the edge of the bristol board, then mark each hole on the tissue box. Push a brass fastener through each point from inside the box. Fold back the fastener to hold the bristol board in place.

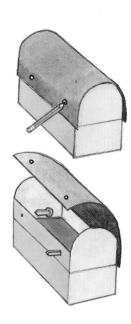

Woven box

Try using rainbow-colored ribbon to make this pretty box, and add a loop to the lid for a final touch.

YOU WILL NEED

• corrugated cardboard,
four pieces each 10 cm x 10 cm
(4 in. x 4 in.),
two pieces each 13 cm x 13 cm
(5 in. x 5 in.),
one piece 14 cm x 14 cm
(5 ½ in. x 5 ½ in.)

• 2 different colored pieces
of 2 cm (¾ in.) wide ribbon,
one piece 3.8 m (12 ½ ft.),
one piece 4.5 m (15 ft.)

• a sheet of gift wrap

• sticky tape, a pencil, scissors or
a utility knife, glue

1 Tape the four same-sized squares of cardboard together to form a box. Trace around the inside of the box onto each 13 cm x 13 cm (5 in. x 5 in.) piece of cardboard and cut the squares out. One will be the bottom of the box. The other will be part of the lid.

2 From the shorter piece of ribbon, cut five pieces each 45 cm (18 in.) long. Tape a ribbon at the right edge of the box and wrap it around, overlapping the ends. Secure it with a small piece of tape.

3 Tape a ribbon at the left edge of the same side, wrap it around the box, overlapping the ends onto the next side. Secure it with a small piece of tape.

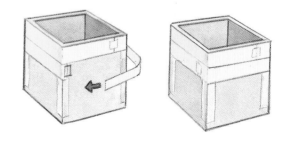

4 Repeat steps 2 and 3, then step 2 again, to cover the box in ribbons.

5 From the second color of ribbon, cut 20 pieces each 15 cm (6 in.) long. Beginning at the right edge of the side you attached the ribbons to in steps 2 to 4, weave a ribbon under the top ribbon, over the next and so on.

6 Weave the next ribbon over the first ribbon, under the second and so on. Continue to weave until the box is covered. Fold the ends of each ribbon to the inside of the box and tape them in place.

7 Tape the bottom of the box in place from inside, then line the box with gift wrap (see page 8).

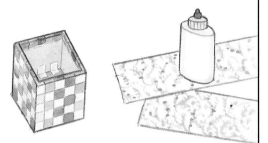

8 For the lid, cut seven ribbons of each color, each piece 19 cm (7 ½ in.) long. Tape one color of ribbon to the large piece of cardboard, then weave in the second color and tape the ends in place.

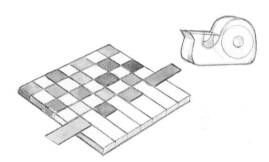

9 Cut a square of gift wrap just slightly smaller than the lid and glue it to the back. Cover the small square from step 1 with paper and glue it to the center of the back of the lid.

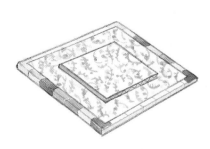

Laced-up box

This is so quick and easy to do, why not make a set of these little storage boxes for your bedroom?

YOU WILL NEED

- a piece of light cardboard,
  17 cm x 15 cm (6½ in. x 6 in.)
- a hole punch
- a piece of bristol board,
  41 cm x 41 cm (16 in. x 16 in.)
- 4 pieces of cord or plastic lace,
  each 75 cm (30 in.) long
- a pencil, a ruler,
  a utility knife or scissors, masking tape

1 On one long side of the piece of light cardboard, mark a point 3 cm (1¼ in.) from each corner. Draw a line between each point and a bottom corner as shown. Cut out the shape and mark the center point on the longest side. This will be your pattern.

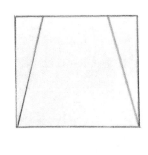

center point

2 Draw a line 1.5 cm (⅝ in.) in from each slanted side of the pattern. Mark a point 1.5 cm (⅝ in.) up from the bottom on each line. Mark five more points, each 2.5 cm (1 in.) apart on both lines. Use the hole punch to make a hole at each point.

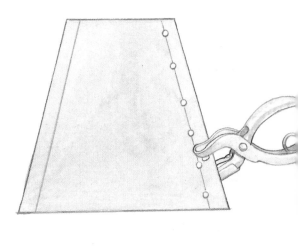

3 Mark the center point on each side of the piece of bristol board. Match the center point on the pattern with a center point on the bristol board. Trace around the pattern and inside each punched hole. Repeat on the three remaining sides of the bristol board.

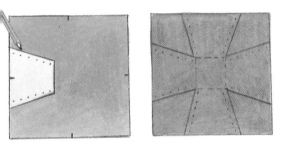

4 Cut out the box shape and punch the holes.

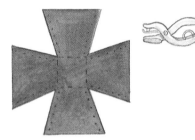

5 Score along each side of the square in the middle of the shape. Turn the shape over and fold up the sides to make the box. Hold them in place with pieces of tape.

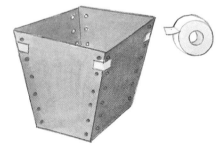

6 Starting at a bottom corner, fold a piece of cord in half and thread each end through a hole. Cross the cord over on the inside, thread it back out through the next set of holes, and continue to lace up the box. Tie a bow with a double knot to finish, and remove the tape. Repeat on the other sides.

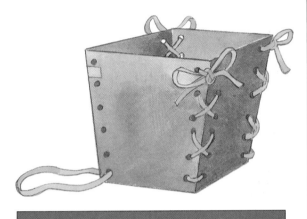

OTHER IDEAS

• To make boxes in different heights, trim each side of the box between sets of holes.

• If you wish to draw or paint a design on your box, do so before you fold and lace up the box.

Garden box

Fill this box with packets of seeds and peat pots to make a great gift for a gardener.

YOU WILL NEED

- 28 Popsicle or craft sticks, painted white
- corrugated cardboard,
one piece 6 cm x 44 cm (2¼ in. x 17 in.),
one piece 11.5 cm x 11.5 cm
(4½ in. x 4½ in.)
- 8 pieces of green construction paper,
four pieces 10 cm x 11 cm (4 in. x 4¼ in.),
four pieces 2 cm x 6 cm (¾ in. x 2¼ in.)
- glue, a pencil, a ruler, a utility knife
or scissors, masking tape, paints,
a paintbrush

1 To make the fence, lay two Popsicle sticks about 3 cm (1¼ in.) apart. Glue on five Popsicle sticks as shown. Repeat with the remaining sticks to make three more sections of fence. Let them dry.

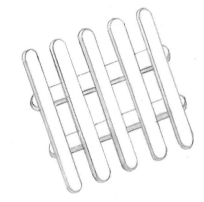

2 On the long strip of cardboard, mark and score four sections, each 11 cm (4¼ in.) wide. Fold them into a box shape and tape the ends together.

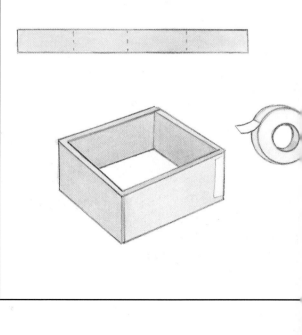

3 Tape the cardboard square to the bottom of the box.

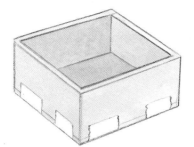

4 Fold each small strip of green construction paper in half lengthwise, and glue one strip at each corner of the box to hide the edges.

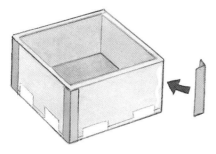

5 Cut one longer edge of each large piece of construction paper to look like bushes. Paint flowers along the bottom edge or glue on pictures of flowers cut from gift wrap or seed catalogs.

6 Apply glue to each side of the cardboard box and attach the bushes.

7 Lay the box on its side and apply glue to the bottom rail of one section of fence. Place the fence on the box and let it dry before turning the box and attaching the other sections the same way.

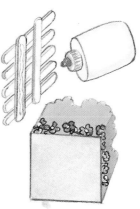

Monster box

This scary little box might keep snoopers out of your diary.

YOU WILL NEED

- a light cardboard cookie or cracker box, about 23 cm x 15 cm x 6.5 cm (9 in. x 6 in. x 2½ in.)

- an egg carton

- a piece of corrugated cardboard, 25 cm x 25 cm (10 in. x 10 in.)

- newspaper

- papier-mâché (see page 6)

- scissors, a pencil, a ruler, masking tape, paints, a paintbrush

1 Open the top of the box and cut off the short flaps.

2 Draw a line 8 cm (3 in.) long down the center of the sides of the box. Cut along the line.

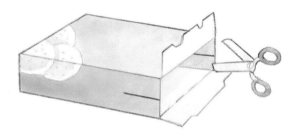

3 From the end of each line, cut up to the top of the box. Fold back the top of the box.

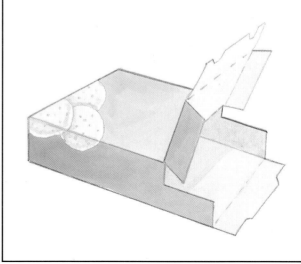

4 Tape the top and bottom flaps to the sides and trim them to the same length.

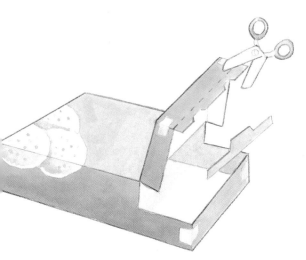

6 Cut a tapered tail and a fin shape from the corrugated cardboard. Tape them to the box.

5 Cut out eight cups from the egg carton. Tape four to the bottom of the box for legs. Tape two to the top of the box for eyes. Trim two cups shorter and tape them to the front for nostrils.

7 Cover the entire monster box in several layers of papier-mâché. Let it dry before painting on details.

Rustic twig box

Collect fallen twigs and make a box to store compact discs. Or, line it with tinfoil and set potted plants inside.

YOU WILL NEED

- corrugated cardboard,
one piece 25 cm x 29.5 cm
(10 in. x 11¾ in.),
two pieces each 8 cm x 14 cm
(3 in. x 5½ in.)

- about 100 straight, pencil-thick twigs,
20 each 15 cm (6 in.) long,
40 each 13 cm (5 in.) long,
40 each 10 cm (4 in.) long

- about 34 thin twigs,
4 each 28 cm (11¼ in.) long,
4 each 15 cm (6 in.) long,
26 each 5 cm (2 in.) long

- a pencil, a ruler, a utility knife,
masking tape, glue,
paint and a paintbrush (optional)

1 If your cardboard is printed, you may wish to paint it before you begin. Brown is a good color to use.

2 On each long side of the large piece of cardboard, mark a point 8 cm (3 in.) in from each end and draw a line between the points. Score along the lines and fold the sections back.

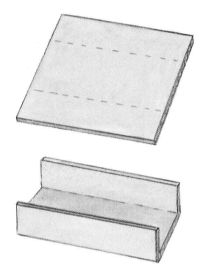

3 Tape the smaller pieces of cardboard to each end to form the box.

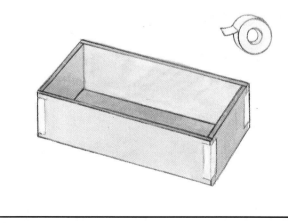

4 With the box on its side, start at one corner and, using the pencil-thick twigs, glue a short twig, a medium twig, and a long twig. Then glue a medium twig and a short twig.

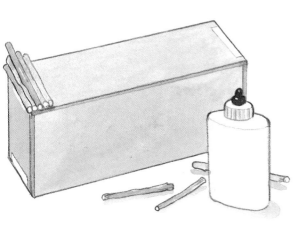

6 Glue the thin twigs in place as shown. Let the glue dry completely.

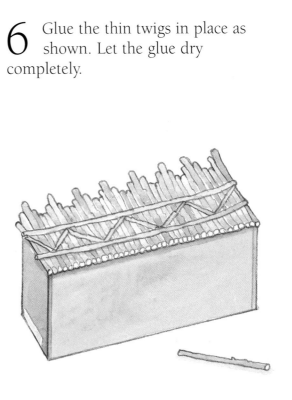

5 Repeat the pattern from step 4. Continue gluing on the twigs until one side is complete.

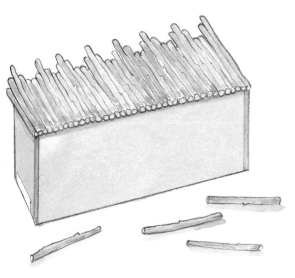

7 Turn the box to the next side and continue the pattern, letting the glue dry completely. Cover the entire box in this manner.

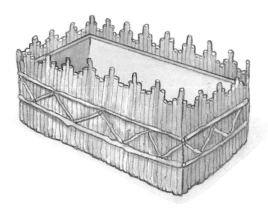

Folded-paper box

*Make these boxes in any size —
just use smaller or larger
rectangles of paper.*

YOU WILL NEED

• magazine covers, calendar pages or
construction paper,
one piece 20 cm x 25 cm (8 in. x 10 in.),
one piece 21 cm x 26 cm (8 ¼ in. x 10 ¼ in.)

1 To make the bottom of the box,
place the smaller rectangle
pattern-side down and fold it in half
the long way. Unfold.

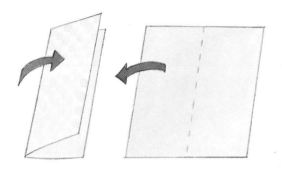

2 Fold each long side in to the
center fold, then open them again.

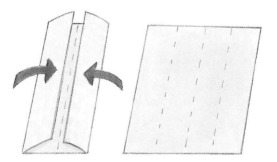

3 Fold the paper in half the short
way, then unfold it.

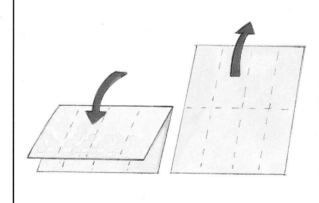

4 Fold each short side in to the center, then fold each corner in diagonally to touch the first fold line from each side.

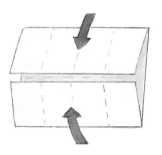

6 Grasp each strip and gently pull open the box. Use your fingers to press the corners and edges. Repeat with the larger rectangle of paper to make a lid for your box.

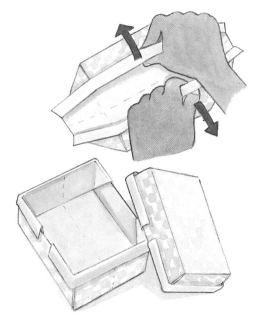

5 Fold back each center strip to partially cover the corners and hold them in place.

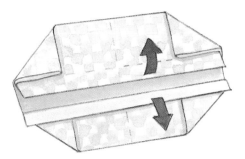

OTHER IDEAS

• Cut a handle from a strip of paper and glue it to a box to make a basket.

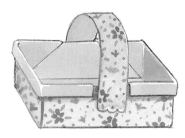

• Cut the rectangles for your box from sheets of gift wrap that have been glued together, or paint your own design onto heavy paper.

Riveted box

This box would look great in your parent's office, on a dresser, or even in the kitchen, full of recipe cards.

YOU WILL NEED

- corrugated cardboard
three pieces 13 cm x 18 cm (5 in. x 7 in.),
two pieces 13 cm x 15 cm (5 in. x 6 in.),
one piece 13.5 cm x 15 cm (5¼ in. x 6 in.)
and scrap pieces for decorating
- 18 brass fasteners, each 2.5 cm (1 in.)
long, plus extras for decorating
- cloth tape
- a pencil, a ruler, a utility knife, white glue
- paints and a paintbrush

1 On one of the large pieces of cardboard, mark a point 1 cm (½ in.) in from each short side and 2 cm (¾ in.) in from each long side. Mark a point halfway between each set of points. Repeat with a second piece of same-sized cardboard.

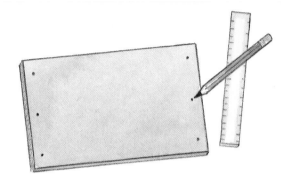

2 On each piece, mark a point 1 cm (½ in.) up from the long side and 4 cm (1½ in.) in from the short sides, then mark a point halfway between each set of points. These are the front and back pieces of your box.

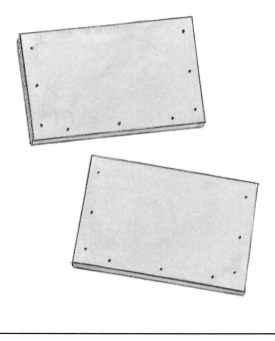

3 On each 13 cm x 15 cm (5 in. x 6 in.) piece of cardboard, score a line 2 cm (¾ in.) in from each short side and fold the sections back. These are your side pieces.

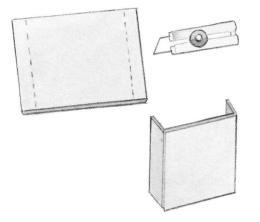

4 Place the front and side pieces as shown and insert a brass fastener, with the flat side of the arms face up, at the three points marked along the sides. Fold the arms of each fastener back. Attach the back of the box in the same way.

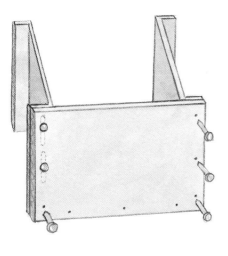

5 To make a bottom, score a line 2 cm (¾ in.) from each short side of the 13.5 cm x 15 cm (5 ¼ in. x 6 in.) piece of cardboard. Fold the sections back. Place the bottom into the box, and insert the fasteners at each point marked along the bottom of the front and back of the box.

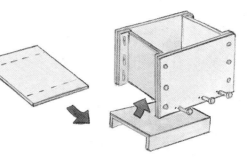

6 To make a lid, tape the last piece of cardboard to the box on the inside.

7 Cut a latch and decorations from cardboard. Glue them in place, paint your box and add more brass fasteners if you like.

Secret book box

Yard sales and used bookstores are great places to find an old book that you can turn into a new box. Make sure that you have permission to cut up the book.

YOU WILL NEED

• one hardcover book
with a spine at least 2 cm (¾ in.) wide

• corrugated cardboard,
one piece a bit larger than the book,
one piece as wide as the book is thick,
and as long as the combined measurements
of all sides of the cover

• a strip of white paper the same size as
the long piece of cardboard

• a utility knife, a ruler, masking tape,
a pencil, paints, a paintbrush, glue

1 Open the book and ask an adult to use a utility knife to slice the front and back cover where they join the pages. Remove the pages.

2 Cut a strip of paper (the first page of the book will do) to fit over the space left by the pages. Glue it in place.

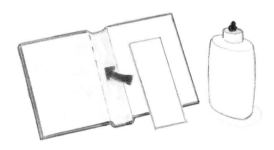

3 Place the pages on the larger piece of cardboard and trace around them. Draw a line 1 cm (½ in.) in from one long side and one short side, and cut out the smaller rectangle. This will be the bottom of your box.

4 On the long strip of cardboard, measure and mark the length of one long side of the bottom piece. Then the length of one short side, one long side and one short side. Score a line straight up from each point and cut off the small section at the end.

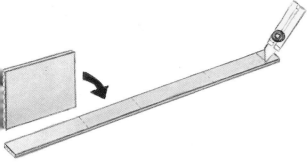

5 Trim the strip of paper to fit the strip of cardboard and glue them together. Use a pencil and ruler to draw on lines to resemble pages. Apply a thin layer of paint that is the same color as the pages. The lines should show through faintly. Fold the cardboard strip to form the sides of the box and tape it together on the inside.

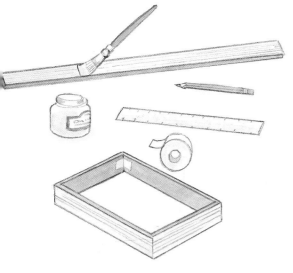

6 Attach the sides to the bottom of the box with strips of tape placed on the inside of the box. Use pages from the book or gift wrap to line the box (see page 8).

7 Apply glue to the bottom of the box and set it on the inside back cover of the book, lining up the left side of the box and the fold line of the spine. Carefully fold your book shut to see that it fits properly, open it again, then set something heavy inside the box and let the glue dry.

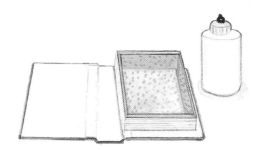

8 Apply glue to the spine of the book and fold it shut against the side of the box. Let it dry.

Burger box

Papier-mâché and paint a second tuna can to make a double-decker burger with two compartments for storing things.

YOU WILL NEED

- a small empty can, the size of a tuna can
- a piece of corrugated cardboard larger than the can
- a sheet of newspaper
- 3 sheets of tissue paper
- papier-mâché paste (see page 6)
- a 9 cm (3½ in.) Styrofoam ball
- one piece each of red, green, orange and white felt, each 15 cm x 15 cm (6 in. x 6 in.)
- a pencil, scissors, masking tape, a paintbrush, paints, glue

1 Place the can on the cardboard and trace around it. Cut out the circle and set it aside.

2 Tear a 30 cm x 30 cm (12 in. x 12 in.) square from the newspaper and scrunch it up into a 2.5 cm (1 in.) thick roll. Tape the roll around the can, just below the rim.

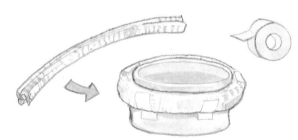

3 Tear the tissue paper into small strips and use the brush and paste to apply one or two layers, neatly wrapping a layer over the rim and inside the can. Be careful of any sharp edges on the can. Let it dry.

4 Cut the Styrofoam ball in half. Cover one half in several layers of tissue-paper strips and paste. Let it dry.

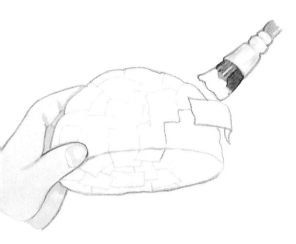

6 Cut the red, orange and green pieces of felt to look like ketchup, cheese and lettuce. Glue them to the bottom of the Styrofoam bun. Cut sesame seeds from the white felt and glue them to the top of the bun.

5 Paint the Styrofoam ball and the bottom half of the can to look like a hamburger bun. Paint the top half of the can to look like a burger.

7 Insert the cardboard circle into the can to check that it fits and trim it if necessary. Glue the circle to the bottom of the Styrofoam bun, let it dry, then paint it to look like an onion slice. Set the bun lid on top of the burger box.

Little house box

A row of these tiny houses looks great on a bookshelf. Or, fill one with candy or potpourri and give it as a housewarming present.

YOU WILL NEED

- a clean, small milk or juice container
- medium sandpaper
- scraps of corrugated cardboard
- papier-mâché paste (see page 6)
- 2 sheets of tissue paper
- a darning needle and strong thread
- a shank button
- a piece of elastic thread, 10 cm (4 in.) long
- masking tape, scissors, paints, a paintbrush, a pen, glue

1 Use sandpaper to rough up the waxy coating on the container, so the papier-mâché will stick to it.

2 Tape the spout shut, and cover the indents at the top of the container with several pieces of tape.

3 Make a straight cut on three sides of the container as shown.

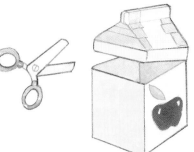

4 To make a chimney, cut two small rectangles from the corrugated cardboard and tape them to the roof. For steps, tape a small cardboard rectangle onto a slightly larger rectangle and tape them to the front of the container.

5 Fold open the container and apply two layers of tissue-paper strips and paste to the areas above and below the fold. Do not cover the fold line.

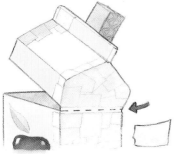

6 Continue to cover the container, chimney and steps with layers of tissue-paper strips, neatly wrapping the edges of the opening. Let the house dry.

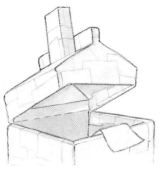

7 Paint the box. Use a pen to draw on details such as doors, windows and shingles, then paint them in.

8 To make a clasp, ask an adult to push the needle and thread through the top of the box, thread the button on, push the needle back through and pull the button tight. Pass the needle back through the button twice, tie a knot, trim the thread and secure the knot with glue.

9 Fold the elastic thread in half and tie a knot to create a loop. Place the loop over the button and pull the lid down snugly. Make a hole where the knot meets the front of the house. Ask an adult to use the needle and thread to pull the loop through the front of the house.

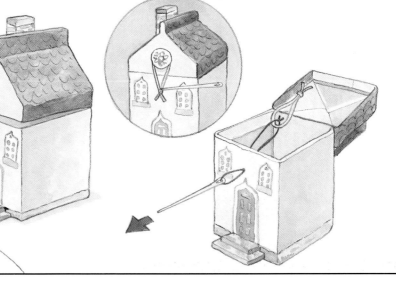

Country cottage box

Make some tiny furniture, add a little doll or two, and give this box to a very special friend.

YOU WILL NEED

- corrugated cardboard, one piece 29 cm x 53 cm (11½ in. x 20½ in.), one piece 15 cm x 20 cm (6 in. x 8 in.)
- 14 pieces of light cardboard, each 2.5 cm x 15 cm (1 in. x 6 in.)
- papier-mâché paste (see page 6)
- 4 sheets of tissue paper
- a pencil, a ruler, a utility knife or scissors, glue, masking tape, a paintbrush, paints

1 Draw the cottage pattern using the measurements given (see page 40) onto the large piece of cardboard. Cut out the pattern and score along the dotted lines.

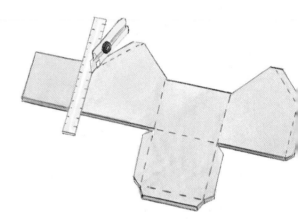

2 Fold along the scored lines to create the cottage shape. Spread glue on the wall and floor section tabs and tape the box together where the sides join. Let the glue dry.

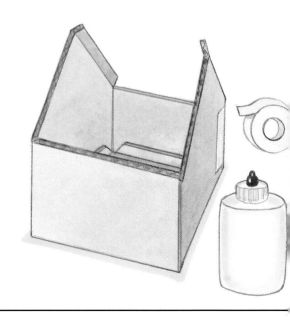

3 From the leftover cardboard, cut out small strips and tape them to the box to create doors, windows, shutters and front steps.

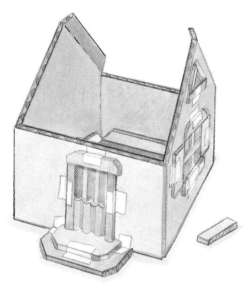

4 Cover the cottage with several layers of tissue-paper strips and paste. Neatly wrap over all edges. Fold the tabs that the roof will attach to later, and cover them as well.

5 To make a roof, score the smaller piece of cardboard down the center and fold. Cut scallops along one edge of each light cardboard strip and glue seven strips to each half of the roof for shingles. Cover both halves of the roof in tissue-paper strips and paste. Do not cover the center fold.

6 Paint your cottage and roof. Paint the inside of the box or line it (see page 8). When the paint is dry, spread glue on the tabs and set the roof in place.

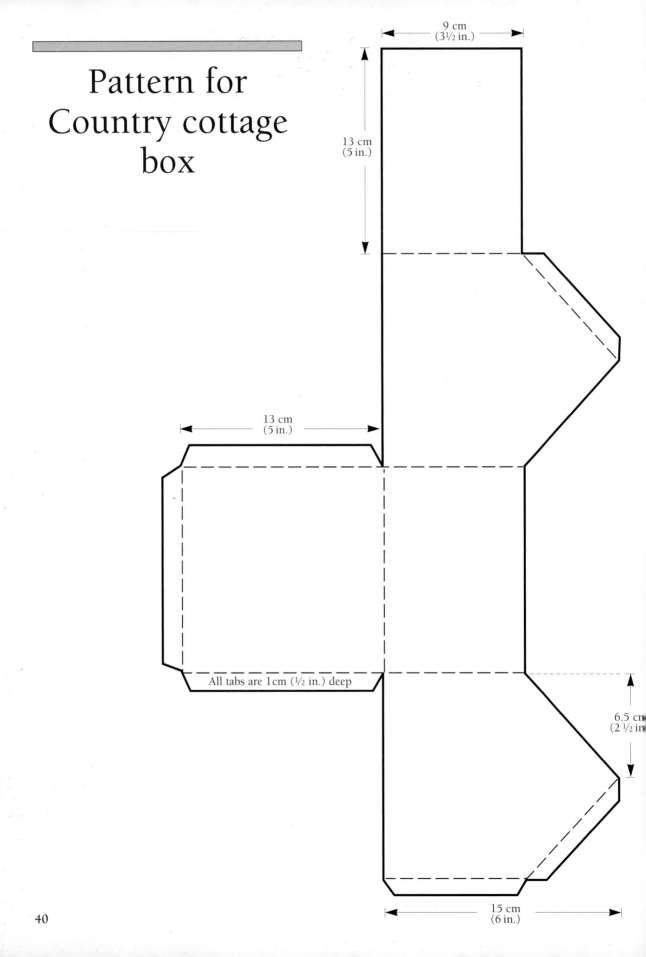

Pattern for
Country cottage
box

9 cm
(3½ in.)

13 cm
(5 in.)

13 cm
(5 in.)

6.5 cm
(2 ½ in.)

All tabs are 1cm (½ in.) deep

15 cm
(6 in.)